Wild

Flower

Written by

April Lee Fields

aprilleefields@gmail.com

Fields, April Lee

Wild Flower

Also written by author:

A Version of You

Album:

Wanderlust

Edited by April Lee Fields

Co-edited by TJ Morrow

Cover design by D Ladio

Cover Photography by Corinne Titmus

ISBN: 9781077679474

1. Poetry. 2. Non-fiction. 3. Travel. 4. Spirituality.

5. Personal Development.

Nanny

To the first woman that ever held me

when first

I entered this life

To the private blessing felt

when, unexpectedly

she made her final peace with this world

And my hand was the last

that she held

Table of Contents

"To see a world in a grain of sand

And a heaven in a wild flower

Hold infinity in the palm of your hand

And eternity in an hour"

William Blake

Stray Dog

I am a stray dog roaming

Amongst these busy streets

Bobbing and weaving in between strangers

Sprawled beneath the summer's heat

A scavenger by many names

Pointless

With purpose

Pertaining

An exhilaration running wild

Within a freedom

That's constantly rearranging

And I glance deeply into the eluded

With puppy dog eyes

My understanding's still young

But at intervals ... I know it all

I howl at the moon

Pant with the damp of the night

But that's already a song been sung

There is an undertow upon this pavement

That even in my freedom ...

I can't seem to outrun

There are voices

Muffled

Laughter

Universal

Though I seem only to bark in turn

Mangy haired

I still wake

To see a beauty resurrected

Within the soft shell of a busy world

That seems simply unaffected ...

By the sight of me

Frantically

Searching

Just looking for a way

For a love

For a fountain

For a sunrise that warms

For it is said

That every dog

Will have its day

Notes

4

Restless Feet

Things aren't always as complicated

As I sometimes find them to be

The earth *isn't* always moving

Beneath my restless feet

But I fool myself better than anyone

With such large, impulsive affairs

Moved by a faith, a passion so strong

That I sometimes wonder it to truly be there

Within this skin of composure

I'm nothing

With everything in between

A woman, a child

Demon to guardian

Awaking within a dream

Sun drenched wings

Sweet lavender smile

The first time never really ends

I'm overwhelmed and distracted

Making

Loving

Leaving friends

I, who have tried so intently to love

At times it holds me back

And although the growth is intoxicating

I'm aware that a balance is in lack

I find it quite disturbing

How normality taunts my thoughts

The norm, a safe and repetitive scene

It's an imbalance I've always fought

My reckonings have made their way through to the front line

Yet what have I even said?

How beautiful and ever changing

Like a snake

These thoughts have shed

Things aren't always as *easy*

As I make them out to be

The earth, in perpetual motion

Beneath such restless feet

Notes

Mamma's Chicken

A soft, smoky mist rolls in around me

Ganja scented breeze

The 'jaaa' just rolls of the tongue

Rock & roll

What is this gypsy paradise?

Foreign music with unknown lyrics

Sooth

Though don't disturb me

With their messages

With their words

… Sometimes I just need a break from words …

Otherwise they play out in my head all day long

Well thought-out descriptions

Depicting a ripe sort of song

Plucked out from

The Eden of my soul

My own kind of self-narrated rock & roll

Maybe I felt it all along

That I would one day be here

Crouching atop of a tree house

Sipping on a foreign beer

Throwing some kinda cosmic fishing net out there

Into the deep pools of life

The bar keeps my company below

Thai reggae kind of soul

A full-grown Python slumbers in a woven basket beside me

Caught red handed

Eating the kittens of the island

The python's fate has not yet been decided

My backpack, as always, serving as my favorite pillow

Lost in my thoughts

Just feeling good

Because everyone around me feels good too

Surely there is medicine in this

Surely

There is

Medicine

In this

This cave has created a cavern of celebrated life

Concocted by true mystical wealth

My health

Is giving me a high five

Bird nests and dream catchers

Titanic webs with prehistoric spiders

Chilling above the bar

Smoking on that weed

'Rope donations needed'

The sign most certainly reads

Because here … they like to build things

And there is nothing quite like this …

This pirate gypsy bar

Deep in the jungles of Asia

How far have I travelled just to know?

That I would always end up here

Beer and fried chicken within hand

Sand scattered and sticking to salted skin

Perhaps all of my previous anxieties

Were just momentary trepidations

Felt only because I hadn't quite yet made it to these lands

How far shall I roam?

The python is freed

Uncurled and snaking away

Making her very own fate

She smiles slyly just for me

And I see …

That perhaps I shouldn't wander for all of eternity

Mamma …

I'm coming home

The Unknown

The air is familiar in its calamity

The scent of childhood follows me

Towards indecisiveness

Your touch, reminding me of presence

Grounding and reassuring

An uninsured explorer

My thoughts foresee

The winds of change

Howling at my skin

Distracting a heart

Unaccustomed to the warmth

And I'm somehow lost within

I walk upon the stepping stones to your heart

And sit down at the door

Unsure

If ever I had an invitation

To begin with

Stacking thoughts upon the pros and cons

As I rustle through my purse

In search of self-assurance

Because I want to leap

Though the side is undecided

I beg for you to take my hand and lead the way

Though these wishes must remain

Within their silent cave

Drowned out by the crashing of waves

For I know that there are things one must do alone

I can't be shown

Nor comforted

I just want you to understand

That there's a deep-seeded restlessness within me

That no love can ever tame!

And though happiness, I know

Not to be perched upon a hill somewhere

Amidst wish-dusted stars and rainbows

I know that there's a part of me

That I must interpret on my own

My thoughts;

Just a message in a bottle

Floating out to sea

Trying to follow the currents

Of what was once upon a me

And I wonder this to be

A life defining moment?

Or just me

Creating havoc

Within my very own psyche

Little green men have me surrounded

With plastic guns and nameless faces

And I wonder …

Do I surrender?

Or soldier on?

Like the little army man that I keep in my wallet

For this is a matter I'm accustomed to

A matter of the self

A progressive interpretation

A deciphering between fool's gold and wealth

There's an intricate world holding me upright

And perhaps it is my curse

That I hunger for its exploration

And yours …

… That you feel the cold and empty draught of my worst

Still, there are parts of me

That you are yet to see

My unsettled

Semi-obsessive dreams

A definition of self, it seems

A DIY of self-esteem

Though your fragility …

It breaks me in two

Because in some unannounced way

I have become your boogey man

And when you try to dream at night

Perhaps my outstretched hands

Shall only haunt you

An invisible

Unforeseen fright

I have gone nowhere in my self-reflection

No reconciliation

Or attuned connection

Just a girl walking stepping stones of misconception

Scared of dying young

Notes

Funk

Drifting through a thicket of thoughts

Where there is a melody

A harmonious vibration

A jazz sensation

As smooth as my skin

And with the grand finale to life's show

Comes a heart wrenching scream from the soul

Of what we know

As rock and fuckin' roll

I'm here dancing

To some arithmetic

Funk

Trying to maintain melody

To disdain

To refrain

From getting lost in the folds of some darkened kind of slump

For I will be

Forever young

Forever defined

For my indifferences

No backing down here

As I have always allowed your company by my side

And time and time again

You take my hand and show me your way

So, I listened to the world today

She was soft in her presence

And I saw you again, I say

I saw you like an elephant in the room

But when I try to separate you both,

The world

And my love,

From one another

I understand now

How I became so unbalanced

And blinded by other lovers

So, despite your permission

I will hold you here … dear to me

In my thoughts

My writings

A push and pull of golden rays

Becoming shorter and longer

Reaching out from within the core

Of all

… That is the sun

Looking out from two eyes

The duality of perspective

Left to right

The sun

And the moon

The heart

And the mind

The spirit

And the eyes

The world

And you …

My love

I hold you all together

In a warm embrace

And know

That as long as this perpetual, psychedelic melody

Of a trance-like dreaming kind of state

… Continues …

That nothing can ever

Upset our Funk

Book Cover Melodies

Rolling of thoughts

Hills

And tongues

Words poised

In a provocative pose

A daring entrapment

Of gently formulated form

Written once upon an unexpressed chapter

This is perhaps where such excess rose

For shown

It is on our faces

The gentle swaying of graces

Or perhaps even, the forced creases of forehead frustration

Molded from a lifelong internal debate

How we give ourselves away

What story is it that your face tells?

Do you swell?

Bloated like death

Repressed?

Aggression just waiting to explode

Like playing cricket with an apple, rotten

... Contact with the bat ...

    Smashed

And delicate pieces

Temporarily take place of the stars

Heaven bound

Do then you fly?

If you have not yet forgotten

Throw in some classical violin

To this psychological scenario

Of rotten apples flying whilst our faces tell a tale

And all will become tranquil

A touch

Of all that is incredible

Because music has a way of making such moments,

Whatever the content,

Simply beautiful

Then, we are like gods watching upon our children

Unpretentiously

No judgement cast upon their awkward pathways

Watching them clumsily falling into one another

Smiling

And biding thee good day

Seeing them nervously inquire to the other

"Can you come outside and play?"

With this outside view

And music to sooth my indifference

Perhaps the lines in my face will soften down

The contempt around my mouth will turn a smile

With the possibility of observation offering remedy

So that I may step gracefully into my crown

We don't come with labels

Though if we did, you would say

"Yours should come with a warning, baby girl"

Yes ... well

I am just a girl

Trying to find the spirit within myself

Trying to find my inner Queen

And I envision her God to be but an instrumentalist

Orchestrating the creation

Of his own melodic

And most hysterical

Of dreams

Lightning Dreams

A seizure in the sky

Allows the clouds

To show their sleeping faces

White light beckoning thunder

Teasing, with its provocative airs

And its graces

Crickets are wild within their song

Singing a romance just for me

For my broken skin

And for my tethered limbs

Reminding me

To simply be

To pay no mind to the ferocities

That these lands can tear through me

And wear heavy upon my mind

To remember

That a genuine smile was once given

When real love was hard to find

Cold showers and motorcycle journeys

I am alive here in this place

And I hope it not to be but a distant dream

I pray thee

Please tell me that I am awake

Like a Man

She will hide her face

And tell the truth

So that you are not distracted by fleshy lies

She will speak as if she were born a man

And words, without beauty

Shall suffice

For she knows that beauty;

Despite its warm and pulsing truth

That beauty is also a lie

Beauty is an intoxicating affair

That holds captive a simple and impressionable soul

Cutting off locks of illusion from her golden hair

Ageing gracefully into an inevitable old

Despite the words that she is speaking

Only the fullness of her lips will be seen

Whilst you witness her skins phantom desire to undress

To be touched

To be fucked

And to be seen

When the reality of this story

Is that she simply needed to breathe

A woman's body is a complicated riddle

That man will gladly spend his days

Such is the diversity of femininity

In that there constantly stands

A complex vs concave

Her hair is long

Her skin; pale as a winter's morn

Whilst she stands and clasps her hands in a reserved tone

Yet, you think them far too nimble

To ever be alone

Whether you have a hero's kind of courage

Or a desperate longing from the start

How could you ever genuinely understand

The truth of a woman's heart?

What whispers would stir your secret self

From such a dormant sleep

Whilst she lie there smoking

Like a man

Giving nothing at all

For you to keep

Notes

Winter's Mystery

Our sheets,

Damp and trodden

Sleepless in their scent of love

Wrestle with bells

Alarm clocks and snails

Anything suggesting separation of flesh

And of those arms

Perhaps only these blankets

Have true knowledge of who we really are

A silent witness to the 2am's

Me, reading aloud from my pages

To your heart

A careless twirling of hair and soul

In between sweat, dreams and tears

I have felt you smiling in the dark of the night

As I have calmed your demons and your fears

There's an intruder here in these lands

Rounding my demons up under our bed

Poking, prodding, needing

A reaction from the dead

And I'm heartsick in this circumstance

The shade of love shown to me

This world in which the only truth

Is that I *am* a coward

I *am* a creep

But I will feel what's true in the night beside me

Breathing moments of dedication into me

Singing, as the season's leaves doth fall

Sleeping bags

And harmony

Seasons …

They simply want more

From the truth that's hidden within me

I love

I love

I love ...

And that is all I have to give

You are the season of succulence

Of lust

And of love

Of a timeless

Winter's mystery

Notes

White Knuckled

I have wanted to believe in *something*

For so long

Something

Someone

Anything ...

A kind kind of word

Or a gentle kind of song

I have needed

My belief system

To take up residency and find a final home

Living beneath bones engraved

'To let'

I want to sooth the scenery

That I've always danced behind

Make-believe ballerina shoes

An empty childhood

Lest I forget

I've been pondering lately

Over what is worthwhile and true

Spiraling my finger

In this ever changing hair

Tracing curls

A whirlwind of empathy

This life

This whole damn affair

Being more than I could ever

Even begin to stretch myself out upon

Still, I believe in it all

All the locks left undone

Every trail of a snail

Glistening

In the cold retaliation

Of a lost winter's sun

And it's in there

Somewhere in there

I can feel it in my bones

The texture

And the breath

I've been searching

All along

Amidst the forest of the heart

Creaking upon the floorboards

Tiptoeing towards my soul

Where not one swoop of an owl will go unnoted

In such a tell-tale approach

But damn, the inconsistencies of my heart

Distractions and stray-ward path

Following those snails and their trails

Winds and gales

Towards a folly of careless shards

Damn not these, nor anything

For I only know what it is that troubles my heart

Disputing my serenity

As you showed me a part

That was yet to even consist of me

So, I'm teetering sideways

And simply said …

… I'm all out of whack

And I am certainly clinging,

White knuckled,

To an illusion of you

Ever coming back

Loved by a Temptress

A fire dancing

Ablaze an evening sky

I travel upwards with the flames

Towards the heavens

Onward and upwards

Past the Milky Way

And 'stay'…

 I hear it say

… 'Stay' …

For this place needs me as I need it

'Stay

… Simply stay …

And all else you will come to forget

In time'

The world's words float around me

As I'm bruised and battered to shit

For I have been loved deeply

By the temptress of a traveling world

Let it be known, she can be the cruelest of mistress'

Been graced with the places I knew were out there

Somewhere

Quietly existing

And now this game of hide-n-seek is dissipating

Fading around the boundaries of my own navigation

Amidst newly formed attributions

I wonder what to do with my life

When the hue of the smiling moon

And the warmth of the Milky Way

Are titanic in their presence

An affinity

With such an engulfing monsoon

And I continue to wonder

How does one compare?

Staring

Into the midnight flames

Singing dry

A heart overbearing

How, to its inconceivable beauty

Could I ever compare?

Notes

Old Man Rock

Out of breath

My bus just left me in it's dust

Chasing thoughts of getting home

I roam

Head down like a child, scolded

Forced to wait amongst my failures

My unending irritabilities

Walking a foreign world on tired old feet

As I was born

… Alone …

And just as I begin to test the waters

Of a self-absorbed kind of wallowing

I look up, tuck my bottom lip in

And, warming unsteady hands

Beside his man-made fire of self-assurance,

I See

Old Man Rock

Old man rock is just the name that I gave him

For he lives in the street right before my stop

And every day that I finish work

I watch him with mild curiosity

As he involuntarily

Chaotically

Rocks

Now, these spasms are only momentary

As Old Man Rock removes his hat from a mat of course hair

Bows and takes a pavemented seat

As if accepting an encore after his fearsome show

He's a rock star, forgotten

A head banging floor warmer

A cardboard box thief of the road

I watch him beside his fire

Face lost in a deep brown river of wrinkles

No signs of eyes anywhere that I can ever quite make out

I clench my brown leather jacket tighter

Against this foreign winter

And, as everything, I just try to figure it all out

Old Man Rock has had his journey

A story unto his own

Although, perhaps his memory will fail him

In the very same way that my communication skills fail me now

If I were ever to venture out of my quiet

And analytical shell

Other wanderers stop beside him now and then

Stray dogs

Extra boxes

And a laughter that weeps out of the breeze

Like a soft-kept secret

All with their own affections and afflictions

But tonight

Old Man Rock

He sits alone

And as I stand at the bus stop, panting

In my quiet distraction

Grateful for this small moment outside of me

Carving out cardboard cutouts

Of this strange new left-behind world

I wonder who,

If any out there,

Will ever miss

His rock 'n' roll show

Selfish Sunrise

The morning here is a time just for me

When the pack are drifting

In their dreams

Or riding the merciless waves of the sea

Here, upon this rock

Sporadically placed upon the curve of the ocean

Here is a moment

Just for me

To look upon the villager, waist deep

Spear fishing

Meditative in his ways

To photograph the creatures in the rock pools

Feeding and breeding

Like so many of us

Just fucking away the days

The children here collect the morning worms

Hustling their beaded goods

Climbing the rocks up towards me

Led by the dream of just one single sale

But instead, faced with my empty pockets

They simply receive my poetry

At times, these unexpected exchanges can be monumental

In the development of ourselves

Other times, however, we *do* know what it is that we *truly* need

And *my* truth is a balance of both spectrums

Here with the tempestuous clouds

The warming volcanic rocks

And this turquois Asian sea

I'm gently healing my wounds

In this little moment here

Just for me

Still Frames

Flash one

Scene two

Ready in …

… Three …

… Two …

… One …

… Go …

And we simply

Start to grow

Do we even notice?

Pay tribute to the fluctuating moments

That neither begin

Nor end

Though somehow, we seem afraid of the endings

Constantly searching for new beginnings

A remission

I am perhaps in

Tick Tock

And the time has passed

"My grasp"

I may whimper

"My grasp on this life …

… I always thought it was stronger"

And before we know so

We are all

So very much older

Lover-scented sheets

Laughter-ridden stories

Mine or yours?

Pictures

With more creditability

Than one's own memories

Catch it whilst you can

Before it so easily

Depletes

Watch it fade out …

… One …

      … Two …

            … Three …

Notes

Flowers & Such

I dreamt a dream

All my life

It seems

Where life

Was but a spring season in bloom

Where challenges were met

In a head on collision

For somewhere

Deep down

I recognized the need to attune

Days have passed

Seasons changed

And crashes bare their own scars

Wandering wild within this wonderment

Peculiar pathways have taken me far

Across lands of great resistance

And cultures

With an age old persistence

All a backdrop against my very own soul

For it's not just the pathways that I travel

But how one is also able to handle

Each step trodden towards that which is spiritual

Fear has no name in this house

It's a mockery of all that love is

An insult to my dreams

A heart completely enraptured

Within the season

Of a freshly blossomed spring

May you always be in bloom

My friend

Moorland Heart

Across the moorland of my heart

There sprawled an immobile

An intangible affair

Where the morning sun

Rose upon dusty planes

Grounds left abandoned

With not a care

And I've been bound, perhaps

As the years have past

Bound by a sensitivity towards their lies

Bound by a deep-seeded desire

For slow motion cinematography

Bound

By an insatiable appetite

Destructive by nature

Of my own accord

You've created havoc upon my flesh

And I can't help but to indulge

In this carnal knowledge

To give resistance and reason a rest

For there was remedy there

In the magnitude of his hands

And a soothing beneath the curves that they followed

A well-rehearsed conquistador

With whom I shall save my distaste

For the morrow

I could tell a thousand tales

Sing a thousand songs

Once the animalistic urges subsided

I could create for you an image of me

But, in truth, I'm no painter

And my words are in hiding

They sit as still as the tongue that keeps them

Taking up room and board in my mouth

And I wonder you to truly see me

Behind your own visionary complexity

In the same way that I see you

Basking

In your own

Unknown inner wealth

For your embodiment is warm and rich as gold

Though you slumber like a pharaoh unbeknown

And when I slumber there beside you

A part of what rides you

When I only wanted to assist

In easing the weight of your world

Lover, fear not the dangerous grounds of my heart

For it's a dusty wasteland

Abandoned

At the scene

And here upon this empty moorland

My secrets are my own

For love

As I know

Bears no fruits upon these trees

Nanny

You were love and woman encompassed

An attribute of the fairest kind

Your fists worn hard and your tongue born sharp

To digress injustices of any kind

For you were a fighter

And a believer

A speaker of the truth

You would wear your face like a boy dared not provoke

You were in perpetual youth

Now I am older

And you have grown older with me

Now I am older

Now I can see

You are fragile as a china shop

And life, the bull inside

You are soft as the cheeks of your great grandchildren's dreams

Soft as the water is to the sky

You were

You are

It's a mixture, solidified

Floating like feathers in a kaleidoscope

You were

You are

We are here because of you

For you mothered us all in your love ... in your hope

We are the flowers in your garden

The rain from gathered clouds of time

We, your children and children's children

And together

We laugh

We mourn

We fly

For we watched you watching us

We grew, we learned, we gave

We became but replications of the love you bore

Such a gift can never be stolen from the grave

Today we bear witness to your dualities

Your fragility and your strength

Who you were

Who you are

Who we have become because of you

And we are indebted in due length

Life is small and the world is large

But before leaving, you taught me one last thing

That *love* is large

And that people are expandable

For I was swollen with it

In your days of passing

However, I would give anything to hear your laughter

Pass through the air

To feel your skin again

I pray thee again

Though now you are as free as the lavender scented wind

No matter if you were

Nor are

You are ever present

Our eternal love

That knows

No end

Impartial Mahogany

Large, grubby work fingers
Slide the paperwork across the dining room table

The mahogany
Is silent

A familiar gesture shared
Between two beings of unfamiliar worlds
And he bids me fill in the paperwork for the girls
For *his* girls

Swirls of cursive letters fill in the blanks
With words such as *Comanche*, *Cutie* and *Rock Star*
Though don't be alarmed
These are the names of the horses entering the competition
Their horses: the girl's horses

And I feel a part of this purity
These strangers, they have welcomed me
Like family

And be it

That I am but the product of all that is around me …

… Finally …

I implement myself well

For family need not be

Segments of darkness

And of cruelty

Of beatings

And harsh rulings

Nor militant

Tragedy

For, I am shown here in this field

Of a golden afternoon light

As the girls gallop faster

Fearless in their stride

A father encourages

In a 'find out on your own' kinda way

His stern voice

Echoing throughout a warm summer's day

His air

Cool

Though void of fear

There are no little boots shaking

Quaking in the makings

Of what comes next

No threats

But instead

There is determination within foot

Kicking

Horses gut

"Geedeeeyyyy uuuuuup!"

They yell, unaverred

Creatures teachin' respect and patience

Learned by dedication

This is what a *family* does

On a Saturday afternoon

And it's never too soon

No, never too soon to learn

That respect can't be earned in the leather of the belt

Nor knuckles

Busted up and unfelt

And food shouldn't be used as a weapon

Or a form of control

For family

Need not be

A harsh poverty

You needn't be plentiful in pockets

Just abundant in love

Though, money helps

I suppose

You can afford horses

For the girls

At least

You're not confined to four walls

Staring at four siblings right in their faces

Disgraced

By their placing having been so very close to your own

And what that placement has taken away

Taken extra toys

Removed any extra affections

A big family

Seven deep

And they were scarce in my recollections

So, lost we became

Starved of perfection

My siblings' mouths involuntarily closed over

The simple joys of children's treats

Like black holes

And instead, we were rationed

One, maybe two chocolate biscuits a week

So, defeated we were

In our magnitude

My siblings

I recoil in sorrow

Recalling that

... For so damn long ...

The child inside of me hated you

But I see these girls gallop by

Some sense of kindred alliance

And I say goodbye to that darkness for good

We bring the day to a close

The dinner table is full

Meats, sweets and breads

Conversations and warm communications

No decorations

And I remember back to my dining incriminations:

"You threw up your rice and your beans …

How do you plead?"

Would speak a father's voice

Cold as ice

And

"Guilty"

I was, always

Of such tragedies

Looking solemnly down into my dinner bowl

Shamed in defeat

The regurgitated mess

And my

Despondency

"EAT"

You screamed . . .

"EAT"

So back in it all goes

Recycled

Pushed on down with my stifled woes

And my distaste

This was *my* family

Such a shame

Such a waste

And I look at this little girl

Tired and all fired up

With the spirits of *Rock Star, Cutie* and *Comanche*

She doesn't even want to eat her dinner

Instead

She decides, deliciously,

(In her cowgirl boots and her summer dress)

That she wants to make herself some pancakes instead

What joy

What heart wrenching pride

As sweet as the maple syrup

That sloppily slurps in between the slices

This young girl

With all the potential in the world

Beneath her booted foot

And without saying a word

I replace my dining room incriminations

With this pretty perfect moment

Happy

Loved

Priceless

The mahogany

Remains silent

Freshman

You've taken up room and board

In my thoughts close and distant

Nestled into that tiny little space that's in between

You're my sure hearted 'yes'

An intuitive step

That last glance

I only wish I could've seen

How does one lose a friend?

A son

A brother

A genuinely loved loved one?

How can we be comfortable with such thievery?

Severed so young

How can fairness show its face?

At this party

Here, in this fleshy race?

Where we're all sprinting upon clocks, hands and tongues

How can we not be destroyed?

I traveled halfway around the world

When first I heard that you left

A silent pilgrimage in your name

I was hunting down that moment

That still framed existence of our youth

Captured beneath a warm summer's day

The careless insects

Our timeless laughter

Was it even sane?

Was it rational to think I could travel back in time?

That if I did … then I would somehow find you there

And I could be checking up on you

A better friend than distance knew

That I could hold what is no longer shared

But you weren't there

I returned home

And you

Were'nt

There

So what happens now?

When the celebration of your life has died on down

When we scatter back to our lives

Above and underground

How can I keep you?

How can I breathe you?

How can I ever risk losing your memory?

So I ask thee

'Stay'

Stay just awhile

Here

Close to me

Be the space in between my thinking

The distant look within my eyes

Be the light that bathes my skin in promise

That you will protect me from the night

And I will wish upon the back of every bird

The feathers

The spirit

The wing

Beating furiously through my trials and tribulations

An unforgiving

Winter's wind

And for what I shall wish for

I am not yet even sure

But John,

Know this ...

I will be thinking,

In the moments in between,

Of you

Remembering your gift

Of unity and of love

Of a forgiveness

I thought not to hold within my roots

The day will be breaking

Birds dancing

And the moment is still

And in this place

Between here and there

Is where

I will be forever keeping you

Notes

Dear Sisters

Glistening into forever

Sometimes just feels too distracting

Fighting for space

Save face

Save face

And I struggle to keep my footing here in this place

I am responsible for my own happiness

Not you

Nor him

Nor any of the words that she speaks

Do I want too much?

Did I take too little?

Am I always craving more of what I do not need?

I see people dumping on one another

'Hello'

Dump

'Goodbye'

Did they even see into my eyes?

I see people healing one another

Lifting hands to the heart of our mother

Lover after lover

Never one moment perfectly replicating another

Distinctive

Even if the same paths are trodden

I want to give space to everyone

Want to see them dance and feel

Heal

Submerge and sing

For them …

For us *all* to be free

What things could I truly bring to the table?

I feel my sisters crying out to me

But I am just not able to be there

… Just yet

I care

I care

Boy, do I care

Please know, my sisters, that I care

It hurts me when you hurt

Those big brown eyes, buckling

Because we have seen the same sadness

Endured the same madness

I was held up there too, for a while

Would knowing what I have endured help to ease your pain?

If so, then I will share it

Then, we could rearrange ourselves together

And just start again

My sisters

My friends

What secrets do keep you?

What circumstances have you trodden through?

Just to feel the fresh breath of a new start upon your feet

Anew

Anew

Anew

Please, my dear sisters

My friends

Do not be broken of heart

Firstly

I shall heal myself

Then, together

We will make it through

Sunset Friendship

What's your thoughts?

Girl of steel

Of feathers, sponge and tears

How far have you rambled

Down this path that knows no prefix?

No anointment to anyone dear

A broken dream

A sewn up wing

A ruffled skirt around your knees

For love could be in any touch

Any mouth to share the smoke

Though how can he smell the scent of your longing?

With a nose stuffed and parched with coke

You're a story I may one day tell my children

When they're old enough to know

When I'm grown enough myself to understand

That there was magic in the sharing of our clothes

You were my favorite winter jacket

In a place that suffered not from the cold

The closest thing I had to dreaming

When my monsters pushed upon me their stories of old

Now you fight a war that I've no part in

I hold only the imaginings of your sword

But I feel your fight and know that one day, girl

We'll play fairies once again in the same court

But since you've given up

Girl, I've been hurting

You consumed, swam in my day and night time dreams

I've been hurtin'

Girl, I have been hurting

Now it's only the shadows in you that I can see

I know there's a little light in there somewhere

Maybe I've just got the wrong angle

We once slept entwined within the light of the world

Exhausted beneath a bed of stars

Hands

Lives and hair

Entangled

Locked together

Forever

In the eternal story

Of who

And what

We are

Notes

Mask & Snorkel

You're deep sea diving, captain

Without a permit from my heart

I show up

Eyes swoll up

And you blow up

Swollen by the kinda forget-me-nots that drove us apart

You're wearing your mask

Your snorkel's at hand

And you've got nothing to really lose

"Except you"

You would say

Swimming further from the bay

Exploring sunken ships

In their fracture

In their ruin

Death

It does something to the heart

Attempts to rebuild a ruin

Long ago torn apart

Choked up, broke up

It smokes you out of your house

Brings you face to face with these troubles

Breathing blackened smoke

Come closer

Taste my rubble

Don't close your eyes

Because otherwise

I mightn't make it out alive

In this sorrow

In this loss

Where a soul's been stolen from our lives

When memories taunt like a child at play

All the innocence that we shared

And you

My old lover

You are also there

Because loss lives together

All in the same house

You're deep sea diving in my open wounds

Discovering underwater treasure chests

The improbability of future reunions

Doesn't make it hurt any less

Because you once held my heart like no other

Our passion, pain and our thunder

But I won't

I can't dare to go under

For, these days, I'm sailing different seas

Lord knows

And the waters, they are bluer

And the prospects

Lean on softer winds

And the swampy waters of your murky heart

I can't even go any further than my toes

For nine years I did love you

Four years I've begrudged you

And two days

Can't erase

The distaste of your ways

The scowl of your face

The feel of your elegant hands around my waist …

The sensation of those very same hands

Bound and wrapped around my throat

No

Two days couldn't forgive the hurt that I simply couldn't show

And 'stay' you say

"Stay"

As we mourn loss in more ways than we could ever know

But nay

I say 'nay'

For two days can't erase the fact

That you broke my fucking heart

Please

Keep your kindness in you now

Continue it not for me

But for you

And walk away

As I may… as I might

As we knew it would always be

This playing in shipwrecked depths

With this undesired length

I always seem to swim with you

No this doesn't make it any easier for me

Deep sea diving

With your mask and snorkel at hand

In my ruined memories

Notes

To Bare

Soul baring is ...

To share one's soul

To undress loves laughter

Down to its bare naked truth

To search softly

Beneath the layers

Soul baring is ...

The faint whisper of what was

Brought closer

To a single microphone

So that a truth may echo out

Like the light of a firefly

Gently adrift against an ebony sky

Soul baring is ...

My stillness

To sit beside an unacquainted tree

Illuminated in its unfamiliarity

Where time resides with me no longer

For nothing

Is required of mine

Soul baring is ...

An awakening

A tribute

To every single moment that I nurtured my individuality

And to every single loss that I have endured

Due to my own stupidity

Though, as surely as the sun does rise each day

I am still growing

And as she lays her powerful rays to rest

On this day

My liberation feels

Not so far away

Soul baring is . . .

A perception molded

Out of the unknowing

An enigma of uncalculated moments

A baring of truth

Interwoven

A blade of grass

Simply growing

Notes

Twenty-Hour Stopover

A deepened purple

Bruised up busta's eye

For purple

Is the color of passion

Tattered threads

Spiked

Leather Hyde

Gez was born with grunge; his mother

"Nice jacket," I say

In a testing kind of way

Dipping my curious toes into his strange waters

He stands tall and simply smiles

Gentle giant walking miles

Stained shirt

Badges

Dirty nails

And right there, upon the airport floor, we meet, walk and talk

As if it has always been this way

Through goggles of San Miguel

I sit at an outside bar

Somewhere in the Philippines

With a boxer; A soft lover

Speaking dearly of his mother

And of the woman that changed his entire world

Round after round

The hours, counting down

Passing time as if it were a basket of sweet dough bread

Deep sea diving

Ships and whales

Exploring the truth to our tales

Gez is captain of the Lands with No Beds

Guardian boxer

We drink 'em on down

Round

Round

Round after round

Meanwhile, a pyramid of yeasty accomplishment

Is growing in our background

Tended to by two motorcycle riders

Building an entire empire upon a tin can tragedy

Finding purpose in their newly formed alliances

A San Miguel triangle of tribute

And these two motorcycle riders

Are responsible for their revolution

"I'm gonna change the world"

Announces Jamie from behind me

With the grace of a pure, flared genuity

I look back

And I see these boys have a spiritual map at hand

A plan and some electrical bikes

Riding across vast continents

Oil and gas *gone* were a long time coming

And, fueled by solar power

They hold their green guns up in the air

Screaming to the injustices everywhere

"This is the end to your life"

Fists bump upon the table

With a passion of true men

Man not disillusioned by the fantasy of money nor resources

Riding for free

Here lie the scientists of a new democracy

David quit his job to fully commit to this truth

He is clear in his giving

And we play in the folly of our youth

We speak of government

Of illusions

Of our worlds deep-seeded confusion

Because we are governed in ways that just can't be sustained

The wine stain

On Jez's back

Grows to the size of a small country

And I imagine the other two

(Leather jackets, flip top sunglasses)

Riding across Jez's back

On the hopes of a better tomorrow

Keeping, all the while,

Their individual dreams intact

Together, we keep our dreams intact

3 am finds our limber bodies laid upon the tiled airport floor
Legs elongated beside the elevator door
A narrow escape after security was called upon us
A narrowed escape
From the San Miguel adventure rush

Jez sleeps; studded belt
To my left
Jamie; loud snoring
Leather shoes
No tred
To my right; David's quietly sprawled out before me
Dedication to a mustache nation
A jet plane fighter, perhaps, in another life

I am protected
A boxer
Two motorcyclists

And me

And we sleep with innocent ease

In the knowledge that ...

We are all in this twenty-hour stopover together

No hotel

No money

No buy one get one free

Just a tin can triangle of friendship

Erected by the faith of flying blind at sea

Laying upon the tiled airport floor

Four travelers flying blind

Bumping into one another across continents

Anchored by the weight of our dreams

And with faith

We fly blindly through this entire tin can world

But oh ...

How we see

500 Bucks Down

Missed flights

Nowhere to go

Such preparations led us here

Into these long hallways with empty lines

Time

Has slipped away

Shiny trinkets delicately displayed

Twinkling their lustful shades

Of desire

Upon your iris

Upon my vision

"Look at what you're missing"

The diamonds whisper to the unfulfillment

In your heart

To the boredom in your eyes

"I will make it better"

Whispered a silken Shiva

Tempting me into the night

Missed flights

Extraordinarily overpriced resolutions

Not even one single complimentary shower

Just a tug of war towards power

And the only goddamned flowers in this man made port of air

Are fake

And drenched in sickly sweet perfume

Advertisements penetrate

My nature

Sat here learning lessons

I can't help but try to shut out this demonology of consumerism

It has us by the hairs on our chinny chin chin

Devaluing humanism

Who can look into my eyes

And give me existence these days anyway?

Everybody's body is just far too busy

Eyes cast down upon some screen

And I laugh

With a pen in hand

For I too

Seem distracted and guilty just the same

But I also see the shame in the situation

That if it wasn't for these materials

Then maybe we would also be a third world nation

Because our hearts are poor

Their ain't no fakin' the truth

That these days our eyes are constantly cast towards the shelves

Attempting to amplify what we *think* to be wealth

And the sad part of it is

Is that we only look at what we are told to see

By the advertisers that be

We only look

At what we are *told* to *see*

It's safe up there on those shelves

On that screen

Upon this page

No one to wage war upon the sensitivities of self

It's safe to buy and to gain

To disconnect from the raincloud of vulnerability

That hovers above our heads

But in vulnerability

Dear friend

I dare to have said

That there

Ain't no goddamned shame

Missed flights

Five hundred bucks down

But my spirits are up

In the affirmation that this plastic life

It just isn't for me

I say

Give me breeze

Give me trees

Give me caterpillars upon my knees

Give me flowers with *real* fragrance

Any day

Memoirs

I want to be written about

By someone with great depth

And a keen eye

Someone who can pack themselves away

Into an invincible box

For a spell

Follow the breadcrumb trails

That I have so diligently left behind

And delve

Deeply

Into me

But I'm not quite sure that it's happened just yet

So, instead

I write about myself

As well as everyone else

Because everybody loves a good tale

And ultimately

I've got plenty to tell

You will know me because of these things

I will sing

Spin webs with my words

And be close to you

And these tales

… These memoirs …

They will bring a unity like no other

And cradle us all

In a soft sort of intimacy

This is my gift

A soft and simple petal

Offered to you

From me

Green Eyes

Feeling my temperament

Feeling out where you stand, too

In your absence

And in mine

Seeing you clearer

With your nervous laugh

And those gentle green eyes

That ask

Simply for love

Kind meadow-like eyes

Thinking of you now

Allowing my mind to completely unfurl

To unwind into our memories

Those large doe eyes just asking

For a big piece

Of small me

You were the sweetest thing that I had ever seen

Looking into that five year old

Frizzy haired

Buck toothed

Version of me

I remember your eyes being brown back then

But that's just another instance of my memory failing me

It's shit … you know this

And I tear up sometimes

At the remembrance of our purity

So sensitive

Two little girls on a nameless bus trip

And as the years have slipped by

I have deeply come to rely

On the crossing of our wayward pathways

Your life is full of fragile and beautiful things

China shop boys gathered at your feet

With the dimples of angels

Happiness looks a good attire on you

My friend, lest you forget, you know how to wear it well

Though happiness can also turn a despair

I know … as I have seen your demons lurking

Though they dare not fully face me

For I hold a torch of sincere care towards you

That burns bright amongst these shadows

I would give anything to that little straight haired girl

Bowl cuts and fringes

The sweetest version of yourself

That polka dotted princess

Who adored everything that was strange and unique

Because strangeness ran in riddles

Through the red of her blood

Uniqueness grew wildly

Through the copper in her wired hair

And because she loved the strange and the unique

That was also embedded deeply within me

Now we are older

Now we are older

And it seems

That now

We can only give little parts of ourselves to one another

As we wake in different dreams

And although those pieces that we've left to give

May seem slim

And perhaps not quite enough

They are rich

And they are dense

And they are full of our unique

And sisterly love

Once upon a nameless bus journey

I sat beside my best friend

And it was I

Who was completely

And truly blessed

Blessed for us to have found one another

Blessed to have spent

All these long years loving you

Since

    All

       The

          Way

             Back

                When

Notes

Melodic Winds

Sidewinding curls

It breathes and it hurls

A phantom riding upon the winds of allure

I throw it all down

Making not a single sound

For there's a precious silence

In the mood of the moors

Kick him on down

Bring her right up

Lick clean my aching wounds

There's a melody pulsating

Beneath all of my burdens

Bath me 'til I'm as pure as the hounds

My tongue swells up large

Inside of my mouth

The heart is buttered like bread beneath its own empty bin

You're a face that I know

From some long ago fable

My once upon a sweetly perspired sin

What silence is this?

When I wish for song

What mockery plays game with my needs?

Grab me up, shake me up, break me into …

A thousand forgotten pieces

For I too was fragmented

Once, long ago

But, upon materialization, the pieces didn't seem to fit

But that in itself

As we expand and reduce

That's just the luck of the show

The curtains close

But still, there's life behind them

It doesn't all end

When the fat lady sings

For her melodies

Her angelic ...

Her powerful voice

Are forever traveling

Upon a melodic wind

Oh, but to hear her sing

Notes

Wildling

Tripped out and scabby

Puzzled passerby's

A melody so jazzy

It rests within the curvature of my eyes

War torn and jealous

I see it before my life

Your strife

How it knifes

Rips through the timelessness of years

You have a gift

Yes you and you

And even you, my dear

What's your story scabby stranger?

What rivers have you walked through?

What abandonments have befallen

Upon the precious lips of allure?

What entanglements have lessened?

With the diligent prayer of the pure?

You, with your heels

In the suede boots and tie

What secrets do you keep?

Within that leather skin Hyde

Grab a coffee

A magazine

Some one-on-one life

Catch the tram

Break the seams

Laugh wildly into the night

For I am also in abandon

Of a person left behind all those long ago years

All the aches and pains of my youth

All those unnecessary

Once-needed fears

Because we are free

You and I

And the world is laid out at our fingers

Which card will you play?

Whilst you run amok of the land

And planned not, you may insist

But the idea's been there all along

Of your wealth

Of your poverty

Of your silence

And your song

So break out in dance

Cheers in remembrance with me

Swim cold watered frenzy

Beckoning seas

Goose bumps, just a sign of life

Tickled pink by bravery

I'm listening to the sounds all around

Yes, they're playing just for me

Take

    3 ...

        2 ...

            1 ...

                Take

            1...

        2 ...

    3 ...

Shake it down

Break it up

I'm living intimately

Ferociously

Feverishly

A mutt ... Can't you see?

I'm just a wildling from the sun

Drunk on the betterment of one's dreams

Sleazy Stranger

I got something to prove

In my lust

In my moves

When I'm posted up

I've got something to say

I've got good will and I'm trying

I've got lust

Worthy of buying

And, with soiled luck

I'm just trying to make my way

The world's a sleazy stranger

Sitting beside a snow-globed fish tank of a bar

I'm waking it up

And I'm making it up

Walking stepping stones to get me far

There's a vision in my waking

Sidetracked by the graffiti

Disillusioned by the splendored rain

I'm dancing around and smiling

At these cautious glances

Twirling against the hushed lullabies

Of yesterday

Acting out

Impractically

You will hear me shout

"She was just cradling a light that I simply needed to see,

You said you will love me boy forever

But I'm still just trying to find that love you see in me"

The sky's a rampant con-artist

Changing just when you thought it was safe

To lie naked beneath its warmth

So it storms

And it laughs, too, in my face

A comedy act of the cosmos

I never showed this part before

To a boy who watches with patience

As I conquer lands I've always dreamt explore

Each step is walking closer to me

Closer to where that warm love resides

Yeah, I've got something to say

Some sort of game to play

Running wildly

With closed eyes

And you run right alongside of me

Run full speed

Crash with me

Into the wormed-up dirt

Cry with me at the injustices of the world

Pull down my ruffled skirt

And fuck me into another realm

Where my troubles hold no key

Make me moan

Show me, yes

Show me that *this* is home

Open my eyes so that I may finally see

Truth is ...

I'm a whirlwind baby

Of touched up strangers

And I've somehow made your heart my home

I'm no saint

But I know my limits

And at thirty bucks an hour

I won't sell my soul

Strangers can touch themselves

Fuck themselves

Their money

And their greed

For while I'm waking up,

No saint,

But no doubt

They will still wake

With empty need

But at least I've got you my sweets

And the sleazy stranger of the world afar

I'll pull up a stool

You pull up one too

For this is our favorite bar

Notes

Algebraic Love

Love

Sits on the forefront of my mind

All day long

Sat up high on a heap of bricks

Stickin' it

To the man

To the shams

To the humpty dumpty spectators

For we have all had great falls

What else do I know …

If not for this love?

Well …

Really, nothing at all

I don't divide fractions

But I understand the mathematics

Of a you

Plus a me

Multiplied

Into ten thousand rose petals

Divided in soul symmetry

Then blown out to an eternally salted sea

Make a wish

And I will kiss

It to life

Lord … help me

Maybe I should take up rocket science

Or quantum mechanics for a spell

Get me out of my heart here for awhile

But somehow

Still

All the atoms and the electrons

Would bring themselves together

In a magical dolphin frequency

Pulsating right before my very eyes

An unfathomable display of God's divinity

Shown just for me

Somehow I would still find romance

Within these spherical happenings

And measure myself up against their curved love bubbles

Emotional intelligence runs me round

For miles and miles

I exhaust myself to no end

So, I entertain the possibility of robotic foundations

Not caring

Just going through the motions of the dead

But to feel

That, it is said, is the realest of the real

Therefore, any exhaustion in this calculation

Shall not outweigh my determination

And so ...

I love fully

With my entire heart

And maybe a little less head

Unless, of course

It is the kind of head with wet tongues

Born of an eternally salted sea

And laid out before me

Upon the soft of your bed

Desert Moon

The Moon

Hovers around hips

Stuck

In his own humid ...

His own lucid

Gravitational pull

Slowing down

Affront with hip bones

They glare into one another's craters

As if ...

They were made of the same fabric

As if

They had seen the same desert sands

Roll through time

Notes

Lizards Light

In the name of honesty

Reflection

And self-preservation

I admit …

I fell like a waterfall upon your rocks

I put it all out there, transparently

All the while

Attempting to decipher

What that mysterious gaze meant

From behind my own shock

Unaverred is a word

That will always bring you to mind

But now, I'm pissed

And I'm spitting fire, silently

For in all of my well-earned honesty

And free-falling aqueous limbs

I have landed face-first

Upon this crime scene

A reptile's selfish need

For the light

The affection that we shared

Feels distant

Aged long ago

For our warmth has been extinguished

By you and I both

We've got our own reasons lined right up to the brim

Though your negligence sits deep

And I see you as a cold blooded lizard

Just basking in my whims

You could have stopped me before it came to this

Could have used your word box

And simply said

"Hey April, please don't waste your time

You could never really be mine

I'm all love

But somehow

My heart is still dead"

I could have dealt with that honesty a little better

But it's not gone down like that

Instead ...

You curiously watched me climb the summit to your heart

Closed mouth

Watched me sweat

Watched me fret

Watched me scream out in love

You just watched me

Fall right apart

Now, I think of your face

Displaced with disgrace

And I wonder how you can be such a sponge

"Just a reflection." you say

In a cold-hearted way

And I beg you grow some fucking balls

And use tongue

She could never love you like I

And you could never love me

Like him

But you could have at least

Wanted to fucking try

Fungi Fade

How many times can I unravel?

Re-travel

Back and forth through these Paper Mache hearts

Running wild through the woods

Rolling down hills

Being pulled

Pulled apart

Until we are simply swallowed back up

By the start

Dizzy and circular

Trying to pinpoint my power

Closed eyes chasing thoughts

And they're gone

Just as soon as I had it all figured out

Just as soon as the puzzles clicked

Tick tick

Come hitch

A ride with me

I don't have but a clue

I got love

Too much

Too little

And if it's all about love

Then how can I not be consumed?

How the heights they get higher

And the smiles, cracking wider

And my laughing bones

Are all tired

Out

I scream into the wind

Into the black cat

Beneath my skin

"I am raggedy

    Scratch me

        I'm all itchy with anticipation"

Where is my strength?

I felt it so raw just hours before

I came up for air

And my underwater sea castle

Well ... it just disappeared

And I miss what was never really there

The ocean is endless with its different shades of blue

And you

And you

And you, and you

You are the shades that I have become lost within

Casting shadows upon my face

Across the ripples in my heart

The light was so very bright

How did it suddenly become so dark?

Comedown

Meltdown

Fool around in it all

The center

The light

Transitioning into nothing

No fight

No flight

Show me again

Please …

Just show me the light

We've got nothing in common

Nothing at all

Not even one conversation

It's my realization

That I see me alone

For I don't own

Anything at all

Not even my words are my own

They're yours and they're his

And they're hers

And it's

Just a little bit of everybody

Squashed into some time capsulated mushroom tribe

Piled bodies upon bodies

Can you hear me sing?

I can hear you and you

And, double-visioned

I see you

Yes, I see you twice

But with all this movement around me

I'm thinking of an exit stage right

Maybe I could disappear

Just like you do

And fade away quietly

Into the night

Notes

Reeta

Dawn breaks through the darkness

Just in time for us to break through

The servitude of our youth

Dust particles shine upon fragmented friendships

Although

We know this one to be true

For those that grow together

Stay together

Expanding in our dreams

Swelling large like laughing balloons

When there was just you and me

Night time would find us

How often we were carried away with the light of the moon

For those were our forever symbols

Solar and lunar

Floating high above it all

Creating a spherical magic

Relinquishing outdated ideas

When both of us

Had just about had it

Holding a stick up at the cross section of Creation and Growth

Guns pointed at jealousy and misunderstanding

Screaming

'Let

      Them

            Go'

Let them go

It was hit and miss there for awhile

A mirror's reflection

Mostly, in that touch of confrontation

It was those parts of me that I simply didn't like seeing

Because somehow you were me

And I would be you

Reflected in the still waters of the sea

We would be wrapped up in the night

Everything about us, entangled

In a veiled topsy-turvy

Kind of speak-easy

And I could never quite tell where I began and you would end

The caramels of our skin

Slowly shifting to a dark bohemian kind of sin

The sweetness of played words

Running into one another

You and I

We were a poetic waltz like no other

Mouth to mouth

Where the blonde fizz of our hairs

Would spark a jolt of electricity straight into the heart

You were my long lost sister

Right from the very start

I sing a song of six pence

All this time later

As she walks tentatively towards me;

Eyes sparkling like a mermaid lagoon

Guitar strapped upon the black of her back

And how the sun-kissed hearts they do swoon

For today, my girl Reeta

She puts it all behind her

As she is in her essence of truth

She is quiet and she is kind

And she has the same sensitivities as I

She can be drowned out

In the extremities of those just passing by

So surface, my friend

Surface proudly awhile

Let the curve of your hips

Keep sturdy foot

Connect and ground deeply

To the core of your youth

And when you look towards the blinding sun

Know that she is always smiling down

Without judgement

Upon the bright light of the moon

Blood Moon

Piece by piece

It fades away

Like the thumb-nailed trail of a God

Splintered

Chipped on down

And shard by shard

It reflects sun's rays

With ease

With not a wasted sound

The moon is thirsty as my heart

The surface

Clouded as a thought

Though it's hard to see

I *feel* it's red

As my blood is vialed

And store bought

A romanticized moon

In our house of signs

It is as opposite as our glimmering eyes

I have worn a mask for some long years

And the shadows

Well ... they only come out at night

'Fight'

It says

For independence

'Fight'

It whispers

'For love'

For when the ruins have shed their tears

Leaving only rubble and rock

What appointment can I make with myself?

To explain to myself

To restrain my known self?

What words of moonlight will speak to me?

When I've chipped away at every inch of light

When I've busted through fabricated seams

It seems

I will have no fall back mat

No sack of sappy

Tipsy-turvey

Toppled true

I am the river

I am the rock

But how could I have ever known it was birthed anew

A stew

Of decaffeinated dreams

Keeps me up

Runs amok

You've been hovering above my thoughts

Like a raincloud

Stormed lightening a tip of tops

Damp and nourished

Rebirth flourished

And who are you to know me not!

Who am I to push and pull?

Heaving leavers of the soul

Sweating dust and rhymes around

A thick and thinned out skull

I am in between and cast of half

A willow once wept upon my woes

Showed me that the picture stretched further

Then I could ever think to know

So I run down

Shun sound

Skeptically skip around my surround sound

'Shhhh' ... it's up

Nay, it's down

And frowns

Were never a crown

That I did want

I ached

As a shake

Took deep urging base

It erased

That God-like lie

That the king placed upon *now*

So it's merging into words

And it's bubbling up

Blowing blowholes

With no bounds

Yes, I want your attentions

Though there are two of my needs

And the cut

Can't be made by the proud

HOW LOUD

Must it be?

For you to just see

Must it dance out loud into face at all times?

Must a plate of played games

Be feasted by beasts

And torn, war lorn

By the saints with no names?

The sun

Makes not a sound

It's in all that I *feel*

All that's red, raw and real

Where the moon gallops with dishes

Cows wed merrily with spoons

Fiddles diddle

With philosophies of steel

For silver is the hour

Of mirrors and of power

But how learned are we

Of what is real?

Therefore, I shall howl into the moon

With these fiddles atop spoon

And release *want*

Like a child to the world

The crowns ...

They will be burnt

And the ashes,

In turn,

Shall be fit to bathe the rising of a Phoenix

In all thereafter

That unfurls

Notes

Pagan Silk

Petals

Blue as the bluebells

Pressed by a bruised kind of violet

In between my thighs

Smudged

Daydreaming eyes

Cast upon a swirling Milky Way

The wind, teasing the milk out of my skin

With a wild pagan silk

Dancing nude in the streets

Oh how the sky doth weep

And seek

Do I

That bruised purple petal

Pressed blue

By a sweetly rouged thigh

Droplets are swollen

Within the silks of me

Rinse it all away

Reconnected affinity

For dare dream do we ...

Soul sorcerers

Dare we dream

Just one more day?

Holy WoMen

The words 'holy men'
Sit upon my tongue like a foreign flavor

Sifting through a friend's photographs of India
I see a caption entitled 'holy men'

A bunch of guys sat, cross-legged
Upon a filthy tiled floor
Blood-orange turbans
Resting upon the crown of their heads
A familiar gaze of peace
Creasing the apples in their eyes

And I wonder, what has happened to my culture's holy men?
To my culture's holy women?

The closest thing
That springs
To mind
Is a pastor or a priest; teeth smiling like a car wreck

As they ask for more and more

Preaching re-fabrications of someone else's journey

But what about just being?

A celestial being?

My throat is filled with shoved material

A lady grabbed my hand today

Whilst I was in the midst of a jovial conversation

She hardened

And seethed

That from the minute I was born

'Til the minute that I die

(Her grip, tightening as she went on to mention)

That God has *everything* planned out for me

My smile fell at such a concept

A bearded man in the sky navigating the entirety of my life

Is as appealing to me as hemorrhoids

On a roller coaster ride

Would it not be half and half?

As everything else is in the scales of balance

Half, some form of predestined pit stop

Formulated by things higher than ourselves

Brought to a boardroom up in the sky

Put to the committee of the higher versions of yourself

Then, the other half;

Your worldly self

Taking responsibility

For what it is that he or she has created within this life

Not pointing a finger up to the beard in the sky

Over what he has done to him or to her ... and why

What about our accountability of the self?

What have *I* done to get *me* here?

What have *I* done to be so completely riddled

With such anxiety and such fear?

Holy men

Church abiding citizens

All so tangled up in my cultures love for money

Make an offering to the church

With its gold trimmed toilette seats

An offering to the pastor

With his gold trimmed teeth

What about devotion to something truly holy?

Something that doesn't derive from money

Maybe there can be no holy men in my culture

Because the closest thing we now have to a God

Is the friendly bank teller

In his beautifully constructed building

We fall at its feet in worship

My cultures God; the bank teller

Telling you that you can trust in him

Based upon the face of every single note that he deals

Reminding you that your trust is the furthest thing from sin

The closest thing we now have to devotion

Is watching the latest episode of Game of Thrones

Each week

And hey, even I am weak

For such treats

Discipline

All in the flick of a finger

Though ... this is not holy

We worship our buy one get one free coupons

For some unnecessary product

That can contribute to our already overflowing lives

So many external riches

Yet such poverty inside

Is it necessary to have two of every single thing?

Two blenders

Two coffee machines

Two more reasons to feel overwhelmed

And sinking

It's an illusion of abundance

We just keep on preying to the gods

And to the goddess' of our greed

Screaming

'Please give me more of what I do not need'

My cultures confessional booths

Are now the gas station public toilet cubicles

You need a secret key to be a part of this society

Buy your petrol first

Then get a wee bit of relief

Grimy walls offer some sort of solace

From a world of outer chaos

You've been listening to the radio

And well, by now you know it's a dangerous place

Because ... well, that's just what they say

Here in the bathroom confessional

It's the first quiet moment

That you've had to reflect upon your day

But you'd better hurry up and pray girl

Because Jimmy here, he's a knockin'

And he's got some serious confessions at bay

So, what happened to my culture's holy men?

To our culture's holy women?

When was the last time there was a priestess among the priests

For femininity *is* the true source of divinity

But how it has been deviated

Who do you think truly birthed this god of whom we speak?

Who birthed the beard above ... but woman?

Why must holy women

Now only ever be depicted as dried up nuns?

With whips for fingertips

Fallen so far from the eternal mysteries

That run through our bodies

Through her womb

Is it too soon?

To say that

Holiness

Has died?

Been replaced with 7/11's and estate agents

What is our obsession with buying?

Our entire cities are built around shops and shoppers

Because, yes

We think that God

Is a fucking bank teller

So, I clear my throat

Approach the throne

Of dollar bills

(A single match attached to my trembling fingertips)

And, without regret

I strike

The heat from the flames

Burns as hot as my heart does feel

Yes … I step away knowing

They can call me Jezebel

Ammu

There is a tenderness within me
That I dare to reawaken
An alternate part
Of the warrior that is in me
Yet, since childhood, I know her not

She sleeps peacefully
Behind a shadow of thorny rose bushes
Past a thicket of spells and incantations
Locked deep behind a secret door
Overgrown with the moss of too much time passed
There, she lie sleeping still

And I want to crawl inside of that mossy garden of secrets
Curl up beside her
As the birds make their song in the air
And slowly wake her unto me
Whispering into the green vines of her ears …
"Your warrior is ready … to finally meet thee"

The time is upon me to rest my weary head

Like a child

Upon the soft of her knees

And listen to her stories of old

I ask, simply ...

That she finally wash the bloody war paint

Away from my face

With warm rain water

With soothing tales and motherly melodies

For she is mother

She is Ammu

She is the highest version of me

And, from this moment on,

I want to walk with her always beside me

Today ...

I place my weapons down at her feet

Happily Hatching

I have not been loved by many

Thousands of faces have not gathered beneath my image

And pledged their undying love unto me

Crossed hearts when I die

No need for needles within eye

I have not an army of admirers

For I keep secrets of the self

Tucked away for the pleasures of the few

And it's true

That whilst I am a stranger in the hearts of many

I have also been loved, deeply

By the red-raw hearts

Of a select few

I've submerged into the deepest of blues

The hues of our past lives

Touching dainty fingertips with one another

Ghost-like

The type of lover

That will explore the ship wrecks of your soul

Deeply, warmly

But when I say to you,

Dear Blue Cat of the in-between,

That watching you laugh and scream

With the purity of eagle wings

That this brings happiness to my womb ...

You need not assume

That there is desperation nestling in between my legs

For I am merely exploring a release of embittered emotions

Living a new life run wild

Saying things that I would never before have said

I am holding onto fear no more

Releasing the cold prickles

That the idea towards child-bearing once bore

Stability

Commitment

Could I ever endure?

So, when I say to you that you make my womb happy

I am not asking for your hand in marriage

Nor drawing up a phantom contract named Forever

I am simply

Completely

Surrendering to love

To all of its whims

And developments

Never meant

To scare you

But perhaps …

… Blessed you are that I would even say such a thing …

Lord knows the hearts that have feverishly wished such awakening

To occur whilst walking hand in hand with me

None the less

The conclusion is upon me

Wrapping itself around me

Assuring me that I will try my best

Not to spend

Even one more single second

In a lovers reservation

No fear harbored

In my heart

Stay pure

My ovaries

Are simply

Happily

Hatching

Wash over me

Dear vulnerability

Even when I am met with misunderstanding

Let me not retreat into the arms of anger or fear

Because they are full of trickery and of lies

Keep me near, vulnerability

Lest he loves me deeply or not

I just want to keep on growing

Knowing

That I can make it just about anywhere

With that weird kinda' lovin' that I got

Pigtails and Afro

(A fictitious tale)

Down in the park

Beside the swings

She sits, cross-legged, pigtails

Enlarged eyes

Swollen inside

Where a city of thoughts doth live

She is eight years old

But, deeper than most adults

She thinks of many things

An eight-year-olds philosophy of balance

She sees the eagle

With two talons

Two curly braids

Keep two ears warm beside her head

Two eyes cast themselves down in curiosity

She counts the blessings

Upon her legs

One ... two

One ... two

One ... two

And, although she started school just a little too late

Perhaps Mummy could have gotten her off to a better start

My sister ... so broken of heart

Inadvertently impregnates this little girl with her own sorrow

Her very own woe as me

But pigtails

She can at least count with ease

No worries

One ... two

One ... two

One ... two

... Three ...

The gravel yawns deeply beside her

Step one ...

Step two ...

Step three ...

Step four ...

Two little feet, with no prejudice, parting the dirt

Making their way all the more closer towards her

And she wonders, whilst sitting down there in the dirt ...

Will he see her tears?

Her childish fears?

'Will he point and laugh at my differences ...

My one instead of two?

Shall there be a mask that I develop and hide behind?

Is forever falling from the swing-set

Simply destined to be my truth?'

The boy sits down on the swing beside the girl

Eyes fall upon a crumpled pile

That's been spat out by the swings

Pale, nervous skin

And hanging pigtails

She shyly looks up at him

He is black as the night

Bird's afro

Black crow

And pigtails, well, she waits for that familiar sting ...

"What happened to your arm?" the young boy pleads

Now pigtails is totally unarmed

She hasn't quite learned the charm

That adults have within their power

Swaying their attentions away

From that which is considered defected and/or sour

So, instead she just shifts her feet nervously

In the chalky gravel

Dirty toes

A heart indisposed

And quietly

She wonders why she was born differently

To everybody else

Looking up at the traveling sky

She mimics her misunderstood mother

And quietly prays to the uncertainty of her fate

Tear stained cheeks

She is eight years old

And already

She feels weak

"I said ... what happened to your arm?" Afro repeats

His curiosity is inflamed

To see such a sight

This sweet little thing, full of tears

And with only *one* arm in this world

With which to fight!

Not two

But one

And Afro can feel her chances instantly diminish

Girl can't even properly hold onto the swing set

Pigtails just sits there

Mumbling under her breath

Of how her birth robbed her of her limb

And like most who have been robbed

She is cautious

And she is nervous

She is eight years old

And already she is infested with the only true sin

... Fear ...

One ...

One ...

One ...

Just one

"My dear, my dear"

Afro steps up to the invincible table, making a choice

Adopting the nurturing tone of his own mother's voice

And to the disbelief of pigtails

He has no further desire to poke or to prod

Or to make names out of venom

Instead

Afro gracefully steps down from the swing

And picks Pigtails up from the pavement

"My mama said that we are all born in different ways

Different strengths

Different gifts

Different beauty

Different shades

My mama told me not to shed tears at the names

When kids call me wire head or nigger

I know it's hard not to hurt

It pains deep in here"

Squeezing phantom organs, Afro reached for his chest ...

"But my mama says we should *all* be proud of our birth"

"Because it's the ones that have it easy

Who turn a sheep to the herd

Living a false kinda life

So pigtails

I will help you up

Because mama is *always* right"

Afro's smooth chocolate skin

Glimmered beneath the afternoon sun

And all that which was fear

Soon turned a chocolaty love

This wild, wire-haired angel

Sent from the swing set above

Pigtails wondered why she had never heard such a truth

As she stood tall

Piercing through outdated ideas of balance

Realigning in her youth

And she played in new ways

That liberated her soul

For the truth had finally penetrated through

Constructed by a fearless friendship

The gaps in her heart began to close

One soul

Two parts

Children are not born evil

And, despite popular opinion from the righteous

Who think they speak in the name of God

We are not born in sin

We are not

Born in sin

We are born delicate

Craving love

We are born a blank canvas

Undiscovered

It is our *worst selves* that do the rest

One ...

Two ...

Three ...

Four ...

Count how you are blessed

Teach your children wisdom

Teach your children love

For whether dark skin

Or missing of limbs

We all deserve a good place to begin

And we all deserve

To be loved

Many of us have been raised by assholes and scumbags

Lowlifes

And cum bags

But brave little hearts always know the truth

What is right

What is wrong

But for so goddamned long

We are robbed of the purity of our youth

So, what if pigtails grew up in replication

Of all the unjust that she saw

What if she bullied and tortured

And pained young hearts evermore

What if she simply became a product of all it is that she sees …

That she saw?

Then never will the chains be broken

Never will she have a daughter to teach true emotion

Never will she be free

We are not born in sin

But in love and perfection

So teach your children where to begin

A caring love

The blessing of true wisdom

Everything else … is just a cowardice excuse

Methadone Memories

Pony tail atop of head

He rasps of mud

And of blood

His teeth; like a merry-go-round

Smiling out an introduction of his demons

Though, even the demon is mortified

And recoils in horror

At his reflection

That was the end of methadone

Close page

The merry-go-round is closed for the season

Notes

David the Druggie

David once met Jesus

As he checked into a mental health clinic

He stood there with the woman of his dreams

Checking in

On a comedown from cocaine

And David had just about made her laugh

"You're a bit slow with the ladies"

Jesus smirked, interjecting

As he handed David three cigarettes

White packet

White smokes

No labels

Jesus talks in riddles

Without explanation

Apparently he has the longest eyelashes in the world

David's friend also had the pleasure of meeting Jesus

She sat on his lap and said that she felt safe

This is David's true story

With or without cocaine

Lady & the Tramp

"You're so lucky"

The words leak from mouth

With no regard for their specific origin or meaning

An intended compliment

Entangled with the unintentional undressing

Of all labor that is actually poured

Into this thing that *you* understand as traveling

You see, with virgin eyes

Cocktails at sunset

Warm linen sheets

Entangled within a timeless scent of love

You see the revolution of alarm clocks no more

Aqua white waves

Crashing upon a sandy shore

Like the teeth of a jester

And yes, it is all this and more

But *implore* you

I must

In addressing the other side …

That is war

Traveling

Is the days, months and the years

Of grueling clock-ins amidst the summer sun

Saving faceless pennies

Unattended parties

Before the journey has even begun

Traveling

Is a claustrophobia of re-filtered oxygen

Swirling around in plane for five days in a row

They call this globe trotting

Yes

This, with a mask and a smile

I have done

And I know

Traveling

Is an exorcism of social anxieties

When directions must be asked in the deep of the night

When hands are held out

Unbeknown in reaction

Of prosperity or of fight

Traveling

Is a stranger

Following you in alleyways

Void of love

And of light

My traveling

Is packing up light

Two shorts

Two tees

Two shirts

A dress

Some underwear, maybe

And toiletries

It is an exiled desire

Of every single damned thing

That keeps me in comfortability

There is no tea or coffee in the morn

And, at times, breakfast doesn't happen until dinner

If even at all

There is no refrigerator in my backpack of journeys

No cupboards filled with luxurious treats

Of macaroni and cheese dreams

There is no needle and thread

To fix my drafty

Tattered seams

Traveling

Is in itself

A harsh poverty

It is the cold of the night

Creeping whilst you sleep on the streets

It is the lion's growl within gut

When strangers sit beside you

In large bellied feast

It is the trampish stealing of scraps

When you think nobody to see

My travels

Are the rain soaking through

Clothes, bone and soul

It is the shivered roughness

Of being out in the world alone

It is Christmas day

Spent among strangers with no home

Traveling

Is a forestry of hairy legs

Pungent armpits without shower for weeks

It is a self-inflicted cruelty

That you have never yet dreamed

It is your one pair of trousers

Being washed

Down the stream

Traveling

Is a masochistic choice

That I have made with intrigue

For yes, after every darkness there is light

And each of these wars carries sight

Into the makings of the fabric of my being

Traveling

Is a homeless man

On Christmas day

Buying *you* a kebab

It is an acknowledgment

And an honoring

Of the strength

You never knew you had

It is a restoration in humanity

Restored against an ever changing backdrop

Of druggies

And men of mad

I am a lady

I am a tramp

And lest I tell you now dear friend

… That luck …

Hasn't got a damned thing to do with that!

Notes

Sapphire Secrets

Living atop of a misted mountain

Mourning the mutations of our beginnings

Beginning to feel myself

Coming into my power

Digging trenches to keep my shack from flooding

Pulling leaches from my skin

Burying animals that were not strong enough

To survive in these conditions

I shed a tear atop of spade

For the dead Monitor

For the cowardice in your retreat

'Too strong' he said to me

But he said a lot of things

That didn't mean shit

I walk away

Gather wood for the fire

Before the rain falls

Digging pits

For my shit

Aware, for the first time ever

Of what I'm really putting into my body

Seeing how the plants that grow from it are affected

What better reason to be healthy

No booze

No smoke

Clarity chokes me

At 4 pm on a Tuesday afternoon

Quietude wraps me up

You thought that I was strong back then

Well, baby I'm only now just cocooning

Gourmet fire cooking

The simplest of ingredients

Becomes a magnificent dance in my mouth

Craving cigarettes

I get lost within the burning embers

Today, a young boy told his mother that I was fire

I watched them crossing the road

Pulling at her skirt as they passed

Making mimic of flame with his tiny little fingers

Then pointing to me

(The stranger sitting alone on the street)

And never did we share a single word to speak

Sapphire

The word comes back to me, slowly

And I recall ...

I am a sapphire secret

That you will never again know

Notes

Perfect Illusion

I have this idea of the perfect man

Walking out there

Somewhere in the world

Just waiting to meet my gaze

Behind the cascades

Of possibilities waterfalls

His love

Will swallow me whole

I will not need to instruct him upon the ways in which to love me

For he just will

His simplicity

And quiet strength

Shall infiltrate me

Sometimes …

You are this man

Other times

You fall so far from the idealizations of my own fantasies

That I think …

"God, what does a girl gotta do around here …

To get some space and just breathe?"

Then

You walk away from me

Into the arms of another

And I am alone

So I imagine my twin flame

Being besotted only by me

Only *truly* by me

I would be his queen

Only by me

He would touch my thigh

Without boyish greed

I would be kinder

He would look deeper into my eyes

And truly see me

But our conversations seem rehearsed

Your person, at times

Is only what you think I want you to be

You try so hard

Yet you try so little

And I ...

Well I don't even want to belong to anyone any longer

You see

My perfect man

In reality

Is simply

A perfect illusion

Notes

Essence

You're shaking eyes

Make not for quaking thighs

You suckle 'til the milks run dry

You face

Cowardly and meek

As you speak

Of your new love

Said, you are weak … not strong like I

But somehow

It is I who didn't quite love you well enough

I, who didn't nurture your needs

When I have given you the very shirt form my back

Given away my very last dollar

To suit your well-developed greed

Cruel, you say

Cold to the touch

Maybe I will be that unmoving stone

You can frolic in fields of ass licking limbo

Alone

And be king amongst the disillusioned and the lost

Even Jesus, amidst the paupers and beggars

Was that of a prophet

Goodbye leached lover

My prince turned ablunder

Goodbye to what could never be

Arrivederci

Dear only

My boy of the Nile ...

For I am always

In my essence

Of Queen

New Eyes

Simultaneously entertaining different lives

Different lovers

You have fallen into the arms of another

And me ... well ...

All arms are wrapped around my thunder

Years of seeing the same person

Somehow solidifies their unchanged being

Being a form a forever

You know with your eyes

It's never too soon to be born again

No ... never too soon to die

So surprise

Surprise

With a new reality

We require a new audience

Armed with a new pair of eyes

To see me differently

To match the power of my heart

As well as my thighs

I am in a carefree bliss

Your crooked smile and seeing soul

You verify that which I thought to be gold

Living inside of my skin

We kiss feverishly upon the shores of anew

And I am a flower in bloom

Once more

When you see past a pretty face

Bringing out the melodies in me

Sing… you whisper … sing

Catch a glimpse

Of this perfect energy

Hitchin'

Tell me I look pretty

Or just keep looking past me

I painted my face especially for you today

Rouged my cheeks

Washed my feet

I also did it for me

But mostly you

Still, you ask me how I'm feeling

As I'm walking away

As I'm leaving

And you don't mind too much letting me go

Your no monster

Your no devil

Just distracted as a boy

And I'm just another girl

That you may never again know

I haven't eaten properly in days

Love makes me turn this way

And you …

You just want to keep the 'happy vibes'

Though, indestructible lives can't be built on smiles alone

What the hell is my next step?

In this tapestry, empty and full

With or without you

What do I do with my life now?

But as I walk away from what I know

The world unfurls before me

Smiles of new are bestowed

And my sorrow is replaced

With a calm curiosity

I wash my tears away

My makeup didn't run

My tears aren't quite undone

But I become a breeze

Drifting on the light of the day

Floating in remembrance of my divinity

Whitewashed pretty things

I'm hitchin'

Going any way

Going any day now

Going all except your way

Notes

Morning Whispers

I awaken to the sounds of drums quietly quaking

Dusty heartbeats reverberate all around me

And soften the racings

Of my morning mind

I reassure myself

Knowing that I no longer need to measure my happiness

Up against the joys of another

For it's up to me to have a good time

Brothers and sisters

Dance tribal on the earthen street

As the sun does rise

Chanting

Dancing

Sacred rhythms at their feet

And I know now

That there is a family out there for me

Don't be shy

Use those feet of forward

And come to me

Some of the most beautiful souls dwell here in this place

Of magic and mystery

There is no need to feel alone

I call these things to me

Fantasma

Half in shadows

Half in light

I write

A never ending story

We are in a tidal wave of prehistoria

Ancestors in celestial rhyme

A story time

Of presence

I sit in the space of teachings

Feeling the whispers of long ago

A vibration that's beneath the layers

Beneath the earth

A look-twice

Kind of Fantasma

Walking

Walking

Until our paths join up as one

And we share our own stories

Inside of this cave

Fantasma

Fantasma

Be brave

Live free

Slithers of slippery synchronicity

"Let's hitch a ride"

She laughs into the skies

Flies dancing around us as they hitch the true ride

Two eyes

Slant sloppily against the amber edges of time

Mouth spilling out into the ground

Connection of sea

And of trees

A breeze

Carelessly whispers with the wind

Says he

Blue hair

Photographic eyes

Craters of the moon residing

In his smile

"I was normal until I took mushrooms"

She said

Pillow atop of her head

Speaking of growth in spurts

And bubbles

I look around and see it all ...

The Green Beautiful

Notes

Play

I didn't check my diary

But it seemed that the universe had some things

Scheduled in for me

As I pulled up to the empty space at the petrol station

Keeping my reservations

For a Pity Party at half past three

Sweat rolling down my worn out body

She appeared

In the car park beside me

Curly hair and a familiar kind of love

Inviting me to spend and celebrate with her

Her day of birth

Clear your schedule of all pity partied reservations

For the mountains

They can wait

She held me with her long sisterly arms

And my diary whispered to me from in-between the realms

Saying to pay heed

For this was some kind of key to my fate

Strayed, I did, just a little

Though just to find myself the perfect passenger for the road

And together, we set sail for Christmas Beach

We arrived upon illusive stepping stones

Soon to be made a deeper secret by the cover of night

My deer skin shoes aided me in a grounding

And a flowering of what was inside

As I made way to this island out at sea

I began to see a tribe

Smiling back at me

My women of Israelite

Whom our meetings had only just taken place

But how they had shone such a bright light

Into the darkness of my heart

Reminding me that I wasn't ever alone

Zested lemon twist of a fresh new start

How beautiful it is

That some souls can make *anywhere* feel like home

With the sun setting behind a cloudless day

I blew away the clouds that had infiltrated my mind

And armed with a returned clarity

I began to slowly unwind

Into this

Ratta tat tattin'

Booty cheeks a clappin'

Sound of music floating all around me

And I fell into song with the highs of an accordion

Weaving

Healing into my fiber

Ba

Da

Boom

The drums never spoke to soon

And I felt every beat of their heart

Ba da

Ba da

Boom

Mouths sang

Feet began to groove

Calling in

Calling in this fresh start

Campfires

Intricate meetings

The climbing of sacred trees

And with a curiosity of my body

He dosed me up on LSD

"Beeeaaauuuuuuuutiful world

Upon which I walk

How could I ever have forgotten to see?"

Then he led me out to sea

I had trees in my hair and we stared

At one another in mild curiosity

Though my heart felt not the connection

Or the intentions of your affections

So I waded back to the warmth of the fire

And was drawn to a brown-skinned sister

I couldn't help but to admire

And as I sat down beside her, we fell into harmony

I could feel the diversity of her spirit

Being carried delicately upon the notes that she did sing

Da da bee dee da

Da da bee dee da do

Of peace and of wisdom

She was true

I melted into the honey of her voice box

Her fingers played in hypnotizing ways

And the content of her words

I felt *all* she would say

So we played

And we played

And together, we played

Until a bearded man beeped out from his box

Making fantastic sounds

And bassey mounds materialized from the adam of his apple

Boots and cats were now tangible

Yes Boots and Cats were now tangible

And just when I thought that, upon this firelight eve

Our tribe of lunar laughter and of harmonies

That it couldn't get any more magical ...

Well ... then you sat down behind me

A man of mammoth proportions

Butt-ass naked

In that there were no distortions

Of what was made up of you

Cielo

The face of innocence

And the eyes of a child

Buried beneath the beard and hair

Of a man

Of wild

With skyscraper fingers, you began to strum that guitar

Changing our circle of three to my favorite four

You opened your mouth and the rest of the world

Save for us four

... It just fizzled on out ...

The variations in your voice

Ran batons around this musical circuit

From sweet honey highs

To the coolest of lows

You transitioned from grizzly bear creature

Into the soft silk of soul

With such ease

That I began to feel your music

Inside of me

Later, we frolicked beneath the laughter of a waning moon

Resonating in new frequencies

And somehow we got completely swept away in one another

For hours

We touched souls

And shared stories of wonder

You became my brother

Of non-judgement

Even my lover

Though we had not touched parts

Just yet

And I felt you to be a missing link to my life

Our imaginations ran wild

Our pupils stretched wide

And you laughed out loud

Saying that you wanted me in your life

'Every single day'

Though cautiously, I tried to fight it

However, my soul soon began to recognize the makings of yours

And I saw us a King and Queen upon the throne

But how little

Did I know

Of you

I fell into the sand with this gentle giant of a man

And felt certain I had known him in many lives

And although he had taken many lovers

Many forms

Many others

Many

Different

Wives

... I knew that I would always be his Queen ...

Just as it seemed it couldn't get any wilder

An aboriginal man emerged

From a traversing of miles

Came out of the bushes

And smacked you right in the head

Screaming, "Shuuuut up"

'Til you eventually played dead

You were humble

Face full of sand

Gentle smiles from a man of the earth

As he told you

Listen to me

Whispering to the upside down of our bodies

"Sing ... angel ... sing"

I opened my heart and sang for you and him both

And felt the dusty cobwebs clearing from my throat

As he danced sacred dances around and above us

Honoring and blessing the love in us that he saw

And by the time we made it back to the fire

I was *forever* changed

Dawn began slowly rising

And, with some Scottish pixie encouragement,

I weaved my words into the ears

Of the few not yet in dreams

Shared my stories

My written memories

And whilst sharing said poetry

I was reminded of my true calling

"I would buy every single word that you ever wrote"

His ocean eyes and ginger beard promised unto me

And as the blue dawn began to break through the sky

And we rinsed away the dark of the night

Whom other than the motha' funkin' dolphins

Decide to come out and join us in our play

Swimming

Gracefully by our sides

Playing

Ducking

Diving

Weaving

Hearing the prickles of their song

Travelling up and down my spine

Magic bliss

How we simply surrendered to it

Aware of the frequency that I was putting out there

Calling them to me

I felt their soft, dark mysteries

Gently brushing past me

And I ached with the same blue break of the day

I look into her pale blue eyes

Full of watery love

Spilling out in gratitude for all that she has witnessed

All she has felt

And channeled from above

And I join her in this moment, adored

Holding her hand

As the dolphins dance

And play gracefully upon our grateful shores

And even after all of this magic

Has softened down and passed

I will forever endeavor to remember the joy of my life

Even when the beauty seems to have faded away

Even when, all these years later,

He didn't buy *everything* that I did write

Even when my King

Has forgotten me to be his Queen…

I will still be forever changed

One little gypsy heart,

Through the pure joy of our Play

Perfectly rearranged

Connection

I am fortunate enough in life

In that I have been blessed with the meeting

Of some truly beautiful beings

As I delve deeper into my sense of self

As always

Delving deeper into my sense of self

I see that there are other eyes residing

Within the depths of these mysterious hidings

Awaiting the same truths

To be spoken

As I

They are other people's sons

Other people's daughters

And I can't help but to look at them

From upon this soft seat of a maternal love

Admiring them in their independences

Even if their real mothers cannot witness it

And I feel proud of the beings that these souls have chosen to be

My friends

I look at you

And see your kindness

Selflessly handmade hearts

From you to me

Laughter is like a Christmas present

That we get to open

Again and again

And again

The greatest gift …

Our true presence

When we are too far removed from society

To be distracted by technology

Where the forests hold no mobile connection

Though here,

We are truly connected

The sun warms the honey of my skin

I melt and move

And I feel free

Conversations are like musical melodies

Flowing soft

Then wildly

Accents of foreign languages

Carry me into the soft slumber of a dream

And I think about all of the you's and the me's

Never a 'oui'

And although I pretend sometimes

I'm not really French

We no longer exists to me

I walk out of the enchanted forest

Where my family still frolics

And I must swiftly transition

From a carefree Wild Flower

To that of a badass warrior

With my wits about me

For we all eventually walk out of the forest alone

Notes

A Frogs Independence

I've got this quiet idea of independence

That I walk around with

Nestled into me

Inadvertently

Excreting from my pores

Eyes cast themselves upon me

And for reasons that perhaps my body language implores

Silently

It says 'Don't worry about me, I got this'

But in moments like this

When I am nervous and sick

I wonder how much truth there is

In this independence ...

Or concept of it

Without a doubt, I enjoy the quietude of my own company

For it's the only real time that I get to write and to read

To draw and to think

Uninterrupted

In fact, I have often set off on foot

In the quest of this complete solitude

I've probably traveled the world twice over

With only my own company to keep

And I find that I offhandedly accredit this to myself

In conversation

"Yeah, I went to Brazil on my own, not knowing a soul

Yeah, probably one of the most difficult and rewarding

Travels of my life"

Do I gloat when I say these things?

My hope is for that to be far from the truth

Because this relationship that I have with independence

Is that of a strange one

Once upon a time

I didn't even know how to book a bus ticket for myself

I was absolutely petrified

When speaking to strangers

My throat would literally swell with fear

When I would attempt to ask which way baggage claim was

Frogs had a pool party in my windpipe

Tears materialized in the sadness of my eyes

Painfully

Shy

And I despised this fear that I was completely riddled with

For so many long years

It was hard to get anywhere

I suppose the cause for my inversions

Long ago surfaced

But all this time later, the source doesn't matter so much

A soft mother

A hard father

A runaway soul, tortured

The desperation of needing someone to politely

And finally give a fuck

Nah ... all these years later

It doesn't really matter too much

In remedy, I simply had to embody an air of confidence

That, at first, was as fraudulent a one as they come

Fake it 'til you make it

Fill your heart with love

I saw my fear

And I began pretending to be fierce

I saw my inability

And so I began pretending to be bold

I assumed the character of a girl that no one dared fuck with

And gradually ... I became these things

Slowly

Even painfully

I began blossoming into what I told myself that I could be

And eventually

I was unafraid

Over the years

I became strong

And to top it off ...

I was even crowned

A Fierce Warrior Princess

Among my peers

Though in my moments of weakness

It is only I who knows of my deepest secrets

That I was a coward once

Now I'm halfway in between decision and movement

Parked outside an unnamed petrol station

Somewhere in East Coast Australia

Laying in the back of my new-old van

With thoughts of accomplishment and of failure

Tiredness has found me

Along with his friends, fear and co-dependency

Twirling my fingers through my hair like a child

I close my eyes to meet them at the door of my reservations

And implore

That they are no longer welcome here any more

But I'm interrupted

'Your fraudulent activity will soon be discovered'

The voice sounds similar to Oz's witch

'Fear is going to get you my pretty ...

And your little campervan too'

Faking it 'til you make it

I muse

And I remember that I have a choice in the matter

That, just as I did thirteen years ago

I can still get my shit together

And walk on my own two feet

The world can be lonely in these moments of the in-between

However, the truest reminder

For me

Is the discovery of these beautiful creatures

Scattered all around the world

Just waiting to Play with me

And I am no longer afraid to seek them out

To look deeply into the nooks and the crannies

Of what used to be

A broken girl

And I hear the quietude of friendship

A rekindling

A mending

A curiosity

And a hunger

Therefore, I make a choice

Without bother

I get back in the driver's seat, knowing

That the frogs within throat

Can live here no longer

Notes

Peanut Butter & Jam

We sit

Surrounded in darkness

Leaves swirl softly overhead

We make peanut butter and jam sandwiches

You and I

We are the only two

In this forest alive

The call of wild things

Speak to our dreams

Singing a quartet of lullabies

Bye-bye, indifference

I watch it wash on down the stream

Leaving just a you

And an I

Now, the dust has settled

The heart found heroic hues

And as my vision returns

Well, all that's left is you

For you stood while my war was thick and raw

Whilst demons slaughtered angels with no shame

You stood in blood and tears and lust

And you questioned not my name

We lay upon the hardened bridge

Our backs to all that's past

Inhaling the heat

Holding hands

Searching for meaning in our stars

We sit with the homeless, you and I

And we sing the Begees and the Blues

We feel their anger raw as wounded skin

We are the unbruised fruit

Shades of purple are beneath our feet

Whispers of Voodoo within ear

Lives lost in drugs of rock and steel

Lives lost in desert tears

Lips are swollen with heritage

Cracked beneath substance and sun

We are the rainbow children

And we will weave this web undone

For see do we

Whispers of equality

See do I

The trouble within your eye

And assured you may rest, dear wounded soul

That I bear no hatred to your skies

Skin

Skin …

What a strange place to begin

Skin no longer separates the tribes

I am a mixture; a dog, a mutt

A duality of black and white

I am proof of this unity

My heart was made from discarded laws

My skin too has endured pure hatred

From a shameless nation without *true* cause

I have been a child and shed countless tears

Though I am of a child no more

I am the pillaging white man

I am the disease of Africa

I am my mother's Jezabelian daughter

I am the vacancy in America

I am the fevered Nazi

I am the lying Jew

I am the witch burned at the stake

I am *all* the stories of me and you

All the stories of me and you

For I am also a white girl

Learning ballet

With locks of innocent hope

I am the *medicine* of Africa

Dark skin; the gods show face in smoke

I am a young man sailing to America

In the search for a better life

I am a golden locket

Within tattered pocket

Keeping promise of child and wife

I am a gun of misconception

Fighting for what I think is true

For I have been lied to, I have been sold

And the same is true for you

For we have all been lied to

And we have all been sold

But hatred ... may not keep residency in *my* heart

For all there is ... is to rise above

You are my brother

My sister

My Mother Earth

You are a refuge of love

And I will *always* let you in

For we have not lied to one another

We have met here on mutual ground

We are the rainbow children

And we determine this new sound

So harmonize with me

We sit within jungle

You and I

With the ground beneath bare feet

We wash in the stream

Drink waters of the rain

And are blessed by all that is green

White

Brown

Black

Yellow

All different shades of our truths

Harmonize with me

My brown eyes see into your blues

Making peanut butter and jam sandwiches

Rainbow children ...

Feel this equality

Harmonize

Just harmonize

Please harmonize with me

Notes

Printed in Great Britain
by Amazon

84824076R00150